MUTUAL FUND SMALL CAPS

THE BETTER CHOICE

James Gale

authorHOUSE®

AuthorHouse™
1663 Liberty Drive
Bloomington, IN 47403
www.authorhouse.com
Phone: 1-800-839-8640

Published by AuthorHouse   03/25/2013

ISBN: 978-1-4772-9669-1 (sc)
ISBN: 978-1-4772-9668-4 (e)

Library of Congress Control Number: 2012923116

DEDICATION

To my wife Suzanne

TABLE OF CONTENTS

INTRODUCTION

There are many writers offering advice to investors, some of them working for institutions who have a specific agenda to push, for example, annuities, or others who for many years have advocated a mix of equity and bond funds. Some, name specific mutual funds presented by well-known mutual fund families, presumably with the idea that by purchasing shares in them you will be able to accumulate sufficient wealth over time. For 401k and 403b program investors, attempting to save for their retirement, the advice provided can be critical to achieving their goals.

If you are dissatisfied with the results of your progress towards meeting your goals, or simply wish to explore possibly better amendments or options to your current plans, you might find the various proposals discussed in this book helpful. Individuals in 401k and 403b programs usually have very limited opportunities to change their investment options from the 15 mutual funds typically offered. Nevertheless, very importantly, they may be able to avoid the carnage to their assets by periodic recessions.

Proposals I advocate, require specific actions. Particularly in this day and age, you cannot make investments, and then, essentially, walk away expecting that over time, they will necessarily bring about the good returns you will need in retirement. A short time ago, many people considered the value of their house to be rock solid with the future only increasing it. The recent recession has brought about quite a reassessment in that belief when values of housing may have fallen by some 30% or more. While over time, prices are likely to rebound, it could be a long time before previous valuations are fully restored.

Some individuals whose working life started years earlier and are close to retirement may well be among the last recipients of defined benefit plans among for-profit institutions. Even some which did, if they had a plan with a company which went bankrupt, they may have had their pension reduced when transferred to the PGBC(Pension Guarantee Benefit Corp). Most companies have switched to 401k plans in order to save on pension obligations. Nevertheless, it is important to add that matching provisions (mostly offered) are extremely important as so many funds have otherwise had low returns. Without these matching provisions, some investors may have had, close to zero returns.

A Short Personal Financial History

I have been an investor for more than 25 years, first benefitting from a 401k plan when such programs were started in 1984, and then, after retirement in 1997, switching to IRAs. By the sheer luck of legislative timing, I was able to take advantage of a very benign market environment when even with an extraordinarily limited selection of mutual funds offered by an insurance company to a small manufacturing company, one could accumulate some pretty good returns through the rest of the 80's and all of the 90's with just occasional bumps along the way.

As a CEO of a small manufacturing company and a minority stockholder, I was able to cash in my stake in 1997 when the company was profitably sold. I, and a couple of years later, my wife, qualified for Social Security retirement benefits. We had no Defined Benefit Plan so that earnings from our 401k and 403b plans were and still are the only means of income besides Social Security distributions. It so happened that my retirement coincided time-wise with the introduction of the Roth IRA Program. Because of the recognition by the initiators of the program that those with what are now called Traditional IRAs could have already accumulated significant nest eggs, one was allowed to convert all of these assets into Roth IRAs immediately but spread the resulting income tax over a four year period instead of just the current year period. This we proceeded to do. Company stock proceeds were invested in taxable mutual funds and partial redemptions used to supplement Social Security monthly distributions.

Since 1997, my wife and I transitioned to IRAs and we have made our own decisions favoring Small and Medium Cap mutual funds, both domestic and international. By trial and error, we have learned how to navigate through recessions and mitigate losses in such times. No periods are free from potential and actual hazards as the prevailing stock markets rule supreme. No matter which equity funds you choose, daily market swings will affect the value of your holdings both up and down. You have to accept that.

Some Investment Options

In retirement, one could invest exclusively or largely in bonds of various stripes as many financial advisors recommend. We have decided against this course because this strategy limits one's earnings even in good growth market years to 4-5% or even lower. I would argue that a more profitable course is to take advantage of "up" market years as long you take the necessary steps to safeguard your assets, and mitigate losses in the "down" years.

Why go through sometimes nail biting periods? The reasons are simple. If you want to enjoy a decent standard of living at retirement can you afford to do so based upon 2-5% dividends from bonds? How about paying for periodic expenditures? How about the renewal of furniture, a new house roof? Need a new car? Property taxes? Long Term Health Insurance premiums and other unanticipated health care costs? Your dividend returns and Social Security distributions may well provide sufficient funds for every day expenses but may not cover these non-every day costs, only some of which I just mentioned.

Your working life may well have restricted your options such as extended travel. Your retirement, in theory, finally gives you the opportunity to enjoy such benefits. The irony can easily be is that you have all the time you need but not the assets to indulge these interests.

While I differ with many investment advisors regarding what to invest in, I do share a caution regarding redemptions. It is generally recommended that in retirement, investors limit fund asset redemptions to no more than 4-6% of the total in any one year. Obviously the concern is to avoid stripping your assets especially when going through a period of potential low fund returns such as those following lengthy recessions. Of course, unforeseen lump sum expenses can force your hand to break the rule. However, what needs to happen is to at least bring regular withdrawals into that range so that your investment base isn't so compromised that you cannot replace and certainly not add to it.

Later, in this book, I show, courtesy of Lipper, the actual year-by-year returns, for a 12 year period from 1999 through 2010 for Small and Large Cap mutual funds. Though not shown, Medium Cap funds' returns lie in between.

Small Cap Value mutual funds averaged 9.0% during this period. It should be emphasized that there has been two recessions in this time span. The last recession commencing in 2008 was so severe that four years later, the recovery is still ongoing.

◇◇◇

The Impact of Recessions on Stock Market Returns

Before the listing of Stock Market Returns for funds, I highlight the signals from both Private and Government Monthly Reports. They are readily accessible online. At the onset of a possible recession, you can observe actual changes in the levels of Unemployment Insurance Claims, Business activity levels, and Personal Expenditures so that by acting on these signals of downturns in the economy you can transfer your assets to safe harbors. By failing to do so, you run the certainty of significantly high losses which can permanently damage the assets accumulated for your retirement.

◇◇◇

A Discussion of Options for 401k and 403b Plan Holders

Some research I performed compared stock market returns for holders of 401k plans with Matching Provisions with 5% higher returns from IRAs (but of course no matching provisions). While the returns from the latter were higher after say an 8 year period, you have to weigh the risk of failing to make that difference of return against the certainty of receiving the matching provision. It frankly didn't seem worth the risk to transition 401k assets into IRAs. On the other hand, the matching provisions in many 401k plans maximize out, say at 6% of income. Should you wish to contribute more income without the matching provision to retirement planning, you could consider opening up IRAs after that point especially with the far higher contributions now permitted yearly to go into your 401k plan. Typically, 403b programs do not have matching provisions so that holders in such plans may wish to compare the returns they are getting with those possible in independent IRAs where you can choose funds from a vastly larger pool.

Choosing Mutual Funds for IRAs

To sort through the many non-sector, or specialized mutual funds, I strongly suggest using Morningstar's analyses which are quite free. You can of course become a member and obtain detailed reports on some of the funds listed, but there is a wealth of information provided which can help you sort through and choose those funds with a good track record. I offer comments on the types of information which are included. Certain funds do better than others in various phases of business cycles. At first, it is a good idea to check how the various categories are doing in relation to one another. You can look at year to date or longer as to how well value vs. blend vs. growth funds returns are for these periods. While there is usually an overlap in such returns in the various categories, it is a good idea to concentrate your efforts among the current fund categories with significantly better returns than others. You can then check the history of the top funds of the chosen categor(y)(ies) which currently show superior returns to others in the same group. Ignore rankings in recession years as you shouldn't be in these funds at such times.

Monitoring a Portfolio

It is most important that you monitor your mutual fund investments on a regular basis. The administrators of 401k or 403b plans provide reports on a quarterly basis. Rather than wait that long to analyze how you stand, you can readily monitor current returns using Quicken or other programs by entering your fund holdings in them. You can check them on every trading day of the year. Holders of IRAs can and should also do so as you therefore have more frequent visibility to change them as may seem desirable.

Assets Accumulated By Rates of Return

In Chapter 7, I have devoted each page to the results of earning fund returns from 5% to 16% for some 25 years with all dividends and capital gains reinvested. Naturally, the smooth arcs shown are schematic and would not represent the real world of topsy-turvy actual yearly returns from mutual funds. Nevertheless, if you are already in a 401k or 4013b plan you can calculate from your yearly investments, over the years you have been in the plan, what return you are now averaging. If your annual investments are below or above $5,000 a year you can prorate by the appropriate multiplier. By so doing, you will have essentially performed an audit of your plan. After determining your current return, you can see what your assets would amount to for future years up to a total of 25 should you make no changes. If your returns are less than 5% or far less than you believe you need to have, you may wish to look at some alternatives. You can also observe what assets you can accumulate from higher returns.

CHAPTER ONE:
THE STOCK MARKET THROUGH THE LAST TWO DECADES

Business Cycles

Before the year 2000, mutual fund investors from 1984 through 1999, typically enjoyed robust returns on their equity fund investments. Often, they would congratulate themselves as to how astute they were to have accumulated healthy nest eggs.

From the year 2000 and ever since, while there have been some market "up" years, we have had two recessions – the last one considered the worst since the 1930 Great Depression. Overall results have been very disappointing for many investors attempting to save for their retirement. If an investor would stay with equity funds as the market trended downwards he or she would lose the accumulated wealth of maybe four or five or even many more years. It could easily take years to regain the assets which were lost in the recession. . At that point, or even earlier, the market could trend downward again for a prolonged period and the disappointing outcome repeat itself.

Let me make one thing very clear. When our economy is truly on a downswing which is not just a short temporary bump you cannot stay in the usual equity funds and expect to beat the market or at least greatly temper your losses. What do I mean by "the usual equity funds"? Size wise, they are usually in the upper medium size through the very largest. The very worst stocks are in the so-called cyclical manufacturing companies which rise and fall with the strength of the economy such as machinery. Automobile companies and their suppliers are another such category. There are many services which potential buyers can and do postpone, e.g. a computer technology and service which would replace a less efficient but still usable older one. At the other end of the spectrum are those companies associated with food, even though these may not be completely immune from downturns. People have to eat – but they can eat in rather than eat out. Health is another industry which is very durable but once again not completely immune in certain areas such as elective surgery.

At such a period, one needs to go into a defensive posture. What that means is choosing the right vehicles for that purpose. I attempt to examine some alternatives otherwise the important gains which you made in the "up" years are largely going to be wiped out, or at least, severely damaged.

You might ask why, especially in the 2008 recession, brokerages didn't advise all their clients both big and small to make changes in their portfolio. The answer is that such institutions are riven with conflicts of interest. What if, as assuredly it would, word got out that they were advising their clients to leave the equities market? They would undoubtedly receive a torrent of criticism from those publicly held companies and investors in them whose stocks were already being decimated by the downturn and clearly such advice would only exacerbate that problem for them.

Some economists and investment pundits at various points in the sometimes lengthy bottom parts of business cycles where there is no obvious "up" trend, like to suggest that an economic "double dip" is in the offing whereby the economy will trend downwards again in a significant way with no end in sight. One can only say that, in this country at least, that hasn't happened in past economic cycles

In the international arena, globalization has created additional risks. There had been a lengthy period when investing in funds of foreign companies actually "juiced" returns because the value of the dollar declined relative to other currencies over a lengthy period of time thereby increasing returns to US investors. Now, with the dollar at a higher value relative to many other foreign currencies, investment in overseas companies tends to be less profitable or at a greater risk of actual loss.

Today, economic events in certain European countries such as Greece, Spain and Italy get reflected in US stock markets almost immediately even when the relationship seems very tenuous to the health of most American companies.

Another area increasingly confronting mutual fund investors is the ever rising use of hedge funds by wealthy investors usually requiring a six or seven figure investment. The rules differ from those required by mutual funds. One of the salient features is the "shorting" of stocks. When the earnings or prospects of certain companies are poised to decline and the price of such company's stock is likely to decline or has already done so, a hedge fund will "borrow" such stock in the expectation that it will decline still further. The difference between the price at which X shares are borrowed and the new lowered current price times these share quantities become profit. Such strategies appear to encourage more volatility in the market creating unease and further selling by many other shareholders.

The difficulty of predicting the timing and trajectory of the recovery and equity markets depends on the severity of the downturn and a whole host of political factors both good and bad and not limited to the situation in the USA alone.

Eventually, the stock markets start a recovery and each encouraging sign typically creates buying opportunities for investors. The Government of the day typically offers stimulus plans to promote recovery. For a sitting Administration, the electorate is less focused at the time of elections as to whether the economy is all the way back to where it was prior to the recession than whether it is rising again at a reasonable rate. The official opposition believes its best strategy to get elected is not to help the sitting Administration by agreeing to such measures but actively oppose them in the name of taming deficits etc.

Many investment advisors state that their programs contain, at all times, a combination of equity and safe bonds. Therefore, aren't you (meaning me) simply making a pointless change? I would argue that by concentrating your efforts by maximizing them in the "up" years (without the downward drag of the bond funds) you will come out significantly further ahead. Now of course, if your sights are set on averaging a return on your investment in the range of 3% – 7% a year and you are quite satisfied with that result, you will not need to change your approach. At the low end, the charts I just have to, show the end result of that approach at the end of 25 years with a set input for each year. Why does so much of the advisement industry push this approach? I would argue that by setting the bar pretty low, they can sit back and achieve such numbers with minimum effort and claim victory. Conversely, if they set a significantly higher bar for success and either by their efforts and/or yours fail to get there, they will be blamed – maybe even initiating a lawsuit.

Since 2000, stock markets have become far more volatile with "up" years seemingly fewer compared to "down" years. Furthermore the "up" years are often shallower than some past years. As a result, it has become more difficult to accumulate positive returns. Some individuals can claim with some justification that the returns on equity funds maybe only slightly better and/or irregular to less than volatile bond funds with far less risk. While that can well be true, the situation changes if you leave equity funds at the onset of recession using the tools I describe in detail and then, go into, say, a Money Market Fund. This way, you can protect the potentially far higher returns you have gained in the "up" years and largely retain them.

While we won't know what will trigger the next or other future recessions until they happen, I believe it is instructive to examine the last two recessions to see what lessons can be learned from them. The first one from the March 2000 representing the beginning of declining lows in the market to sustainable upturns commencing in September 2003 had both similarities and differences to the more recent 2008 and 2009 period. In the latter case, while the official end of the recession was June 2009, here in July 2012, there is still high unemployment and a stock market which lurches day to day from improvements to declines. Investors not only have to observe domestic economic trends but those abroad from Greece, Spain and China.

Nevertheless, it is still possible to examine national data which the US Government and the private sector compile and make decisions based on them. It is never a slam-dunk, and one can keep on learning from mistakes and changing course at times derived from this data. You can be reasonably assured that by doing so you will make better decisions than standing pat. This is especially true when contemplating the probability of major declines in your portfolio.

I will be using the NASDAQ Composite Index throughout this book to check the correlation between the economic indicators and stock market movements because that statistic much more closely correlates with these indicators on a day to day basis with the small and medium funds favored.

CHAPTER TWO:
RECESSIONS. PERIODS TO WITHDRAW FROM AND RE-ENTER EQUITY FUNDS

I am indebted to Bernard Baumohl's "The Secrets of Economic Indicators" whose highlights I have digested. It is also very well written and easy to follow. In the Second Edition published in 2007, he reviews chapter by chapter, various indicators of changes to the economy and how they affect the stock and bond markets. The very first page of each chapter includes the Website address for accessing these reports. This information allows every investor to inform him or herself on the contents of these monthly reports so that one is not dependent on pundits who may have a specific agenda which isn't necessarily consonant with yours. He is the first to admit that these Economic Indicators hardly conform to a $1 + 1 = 2$ relationship. He recognizes that the causes of recessions stem from different causes which make predictions of future recessions, challenging. Nevertheless, while he discusses about seven or eight sources of information both Government and private he finds some correlate better than others to equity stock market movements and, separately, bond prices.

To test Baumohl's conclusions with regard to the equity markets, I looked at each of these two recessions and the degree to which they correlated with specific Government and private sector reports. He also separates some reports which are the best indicators of economic declines from others which are more attuned to recoveries.

The 2000-2003 Recession

The ISM Report – Manufacturing (The Institute created by the Institute for Supply Management (or ISM). Web Site: www.ism.ws: A manufacturing survey which obtains its information from 400 member companies representing 20 industries. It focuses on new orders by Purchasing Managers including manufacturing output, hiring, order backlogs, and prices among other features. These are weighted and seasonally adjusted. It derives its ultimate single index figure based on activity changes from the previous month.

A PMI reading of 50 is believed to be consistent with a GDP growth of 2.5% *. An index change to 51 would represent about 0.3% growth if continued for over a year. Conversely a PMI reading of 49 does not indicate negative growth but a growth rate of 2.2%.A PMI reading of 47 would indicate a GDP growth rate of 1.6%.

	JAN	FEB	MAR	APR	MAY	JUN	JUL	AUG	SEPT	OCT	NOV	DEC
2001	42.3	42.1	43.1	42.7	41.3	43.2	43.5	46.3	46.2	40.8	44.1	45.3
2000	56.7	55.8	54.9	54.7	53.2	51.4	52.5	49.9	49.7	48.7	48.5	43.9
1999	50.6	51.7	52.4	52.3	54.3	55.8	53.6	54.8	57.0	57.2	58.1	57.8

In the year 2000, the PMI fell below 50 for the first time in August 2000. For that month and the next two months, the average was 49.4. The average for all of 2001 was 43.4. That would indicate a drop in GDP growth from 2.5% (a PMI of 50) to about 1.1%. It has to be admitted that were months in 2002 when the PMI went over 51 (an average of 52.9) from March through June of that year. From July 2002, the Index fell again and averaged 49.2 for 12 months from that month through June 2003.

Note: The current format of ISM's Report on Business has changed from the above illustration. You can look at the most recently published monthly ISM Report on Business and the all-important previous month's Index figure is quickly observable. Scroll down to the base of the chart and a small grey rectangular chart appears. On it there is a line chart which shows trends for the last 3 years. If you wish to look at actual numerics for earlier years, you can enter the word "Archives" where "Search" is indicated and you will find a listing of previous years.

Weekly Claims for Unemployment Insurance. www.doleta.gov/unemploy/wkclaims/ report.asp: In the first month or two of each year, temps lose their Christmas jobs and file for unemployment. After that, up and down changes better reflect the health of the economy. Even so, it is better to consider quarterly averages rather than single months. The long term average is about 368,000 claims. The third quarter average for 2000 was only 265,000 claims. The fourth quarter average shot up to 362,000 claims. The first quarter of 2001 averaged 477,000 claims. It then bounced around and hit a quarterly peak of 518,000 in the last quarter of 2001. This was followed by more decreases and fewer increases in subsequent quarters but generally higher than the longer term average of 368,000. See Table One starting below.

Table One.
Report r539cy
Subject: Unemployment Insurance Weekly Claims Data - Report r539cy

	Initial Claims			Continued Claims			I.U.R		Covered
	N.S.A	S.F.	S.A.	N.S.A	S.F.	S.A.	N.S.A	S.A.	Employment
10/07/2000	292,784	94.9	309,000	1,723,497	80.8	2,133,000	1.4	1.7	126,084,568
10/14/2000	255,082	85.2	299,000	1,788,584	84.2	2,124,000	1.4	1.7	126,084,568
10/21/2000	263,445	89.2	295,000	1,753,464	84.2	2,082,000	1.4	1.7	126,084,568
10/28/2000	269,489	89.5	301,000	1,822,289	85.7	2,126,000	1.4	1.7	126,084,568
11/04/2000	342,414	103.4	331,000	1,774,889	84.1	2,110,000	1.4	1.7	126,084,568
11/11/2000	294,727	92.7	318,000	1,972,938	91.3	2,161,000	1.6	1.7	126,084,568
11/18/2000	374,160	112.7	332,000	1,898,521	83.3	2,279,000	1.5	1.8	126,084,568
11/25/2000	321,859	90.3	356,000	2,394,176	104.3	2,295,000	1.9	1.8	126,084,568

12/02/2000	447,262	132.5	338,000	2,211,195	99.2	2,229,000	1.8	1.8	126,084,568
12/09/2000	390,088	121.4	321,000	2,315,331	102.3	2,263,000	1.8	1.8	126,084,568
12/16/2000	402,476	113.7	354,000	2,356,340	101.5	2,322,000	1.9	1.8	126,084,568
12/23/2000	481,720	132.5	364,000	2,525,315	107.9	2,340,000	2.0	1.9	126,084,568
12/30/2000	568,973	161.1	353,000	2,983,919	125.5	2,378,000	2.4	1.9	126,084,568
01/06/2001	558,768	165.7	337,000	3,067,097	130.1	2,357,000	2.4	1.9	126,843,537
01/13/2001	599,562	188.3	318,000	2,833,258	119.7	2,367,000	2.2	1.9	126,843,537
01/20/2001	398,188	116.1	343,000	3,048,535	126.0	2,419,000	2.4	1.9	126,843,537
01/27/2001	447,386	123.5	362,000	2,950,004	120.9	2,440,000	2.3	1.9	126,843,537
02/03/2001	424,696	113.1	376,000	3,052,109	122.6	2,489,000	2.4	2.0	126,843,537
02/10/2001	396,151	108.4	365,000	2,936,361	120.6	2,435,000	2.3'	1.9	126,843,537
02/17/2001	345,841	96.6	358,000	3,003,753	119.4	2,516,000	2.4	2.0	126,843,537
02/24/2001	357,591	92.7	386,000	3,016,843	120.4	2,506,000	2.4	2.0	126,843,537
03/03/2001	379,286	98.8	384,000	3,049,224	119.2	2,558,000	2.4	2.0	126,843,537
03/10/2001	377,210	96.1	393,000	2,966,369	116.0	2,557,000	2.3	2.0	126,843,537
03/17/2001	351,497	89.5	393,000	2,984,895	114.6	2,605,000	2.4	2.1	126,843,537
03/24/2001	334,747	88.6	378,000	2,860,911	110.6	2,587,000	2.3	2.0	126,843,537
03/31/2001	328,576	84.6	388,000	2,844,860	108.6	2,620,000	2.2	2.1	126,843,537

Bureau of Economic Analysis (BEA). Personal Income and Spending. Web Site: www.bea.gov/: While statistics gathered by this Govt. agency can be an excellent harbinger of important trends leading up to some recessions, especially Durable Goods expenditures in Table 7, that was not the case in the 2003 recession as spending continued fairly normally during that period.

What happened in the stock markets? The NASDAQ Composite Index which best correlates with Small and Medium Cap companies' ups and downs had a high of 4915 on February 28 2000. By April 1 2000 it dropped to 3817 (a 22% decline). This was followed by modest upticks and further declines to a low of 1140 (a reduction from March 2000 of 77%) by September 30 2002. In April 2003, upturns started to be more consistent and by the yearend was 1938.

Comment: To put the above data in some perspective, it should be underlined that the Stock Market high by the end of February 2000 was to a very high degree a reflection of the so-called dot.com era when any new company start-up whose name ended in –tech. was automatically deemed a winner. Most of these companies bit the dust when the realization finally hit home that their stock prices of 50 or 60 times earnings were unsustainable. This recognition quickly changed the market sentiment of growth at any price to one where value was much more the order of the day. Small stock value funds had positive earnings for the first two years, 2000 and 2001 while the growth funds all took big hits (See the tables of Mutual Fund Yearly Returns, specifically Value vs. Growth Funds. page).

◇◇◇

The 2008 Recession.

While as I noted above, the 2000 recession was the result of wild speculation in the area of technologies, the 2008 recession was largely fueled by the virtual collapse of the housing market. "Easy money" – that is billions of dollars in credit issued for mortgages with too little income on the part of customers to support repayment. These mortgages were typically bundled into securities which were then traded and re-traded. The onset and growth of home foreclosures created huge losses by many banks whose liquidity imploded. Some closed, while others were merged into stronger banks who were assisted by US Government funding. Many banks had insured these securities with AIG (The insurance giant) who then also became illiquid. They too had to be bailed out. In addition, many homeowners used the collateral from their house's ever increasing value to finance other items such as new furniture, new cars etc. When the housing market no longer grew and foreclosures rapidly increased, house values came tumbling down by 30% or more and many homeowners owed more money than their house was worth.

Let us examine how the stock markets and the economic indicators reacted. The NASDAQ Composite Index at the end of 2007 was 2505. Similar numbers were reported for the period January 2 through May. After that, it started to decline, for some three months and then an accelerated decline so that by yearend it was at 1632 (a decline of 35%.) The decline continued until on March 2 it was a low of 1294.

The Weekly Claims for Unemployment Insurance. www.doleta.gov/unemploy/ wkclaims/report.asp: This particular economic indicator has properly taken center stage as it has become a tragic enumerator of a huge swath of the population's woes. In periods of economic uncertainty, employers become reluctant hirers. After September 2008, rapid changes began to occur. In October 2008, Weekly Claims for Unemployment Insurance climbed from the 390's (thousands) into the 400's. In November 2008, there were 500s and 600s. In December there were 700s. See Table 2 below.

Table 2
Report r539cy
Subject: Unemployment Insurance Weekly Claims Data - Report r539cy

	Initial Claims			Continued Claims			I.U.R		Covered
10/18/2008	416,114	86.8	479,000	3,233,118	86.6	3,733,000	2.4	2.8	133,902,387
10/25/2008	449,429	93.7	480,000	3,310,892	86.7	3,819,000	2.5	2.9	133,902,387
11/01/2008	466,373	95.4	489,000	3,460,633	87.9	3,937,000	2.6	2.9	133,902,387
11/08/2008	539,812	105.6	511,000	3,521,951	87.5	4,025,000	2.6	3.0	133,902,387
11/15/2008	513,047	94.9	541,000	3,781,631	94.3	4,010,000	2.8	3.0	133,902,387
11/22/2008	609,128	113.7	536,000	3,652,990	89.0	4,104,000	2.7	3.1	133,902,387
11/29/2008	537,230	101.3	530,000	4,495,571	IOLI	4,447,000	3.4	3.3	133,902,387
12/06/2008	760,481	134.2	567,000	4,377,029	99.0	4,421,000	3.3	3.3	133,902,387
12/13/2008	629,867	111.5	565,000	4,591,216	103.3	4,445,000	3.4	3.3	133,902,387
12/20/2008	719,691	122.9	586,000	4,566,281	100.2	4,557,000	3.4	3.4	133,902,387
12/27/2008	717,000	134.8	532,000	5,311,032	113.6	4,675,000	4.0	3.5	133,902,387
01/03/2009	731,958	145.1	504,000	5,845,860	124.2	4,707,000	4.4	3.5	133,886,830
01/10/2009	956,791	175.2	546,000	5,650,014	118.2	4,780,000	4.2	3.6	133,886,830
01/17/2009	763,987	130.4	586,000	5,715,432	117.2	4,877,000	4.3	3.6	133,886,830
01/24/2009	620,143	106.0	585,000	5,806,901	115.6	5,023,000	4.3	3.8	133,886,830
01/31/2009	682,176	106.9	638,000	5,952,109	118.4	5,027,000	4.4	3.8	133,886,830
02/07/2009	710,152	111.9	635,00Q	5,971,341	115.4	5,174,000	4.5	3.9	133,886,830
02/14/2009	619,951	97.7	635,000	6,107,800	115.6	5,284,000	4.6	3.9	133,886,830
02/21/2009	605,668	92.4	655,000	6,230,217	117.1	5,320,000	4.7	4.0	133,886,830
02/28/2009	645,827	98.9	653,000	6,359,961	116.8	5,445,000'	4.8'	4.1	133,886,830
03/07/2009	652,635	99.0	659,000	6,356,097	113.4	5,605,000	4.7	4.2	133,886,830
03/14/2009	601,192	92.7	649,000	6,440,135	113.2	5,689,000	4.8	4.2	133,886,830
03/21/2009	590,067	89.1	662,000	6,388,414	109.5	5,834,000	4.8	4.4	133,886,830
03/28/2009	599,299	89.9	667,000	6,451,690	108.9	5,924,000	4.8	4.4	133,886,830

Personal Income and Outlays. This publication is put out by the Bureau of Economic Analysis:www.bea.gov Typically, consumers spend over 95% of their income so that an analysis of spending changes from period to period can be a very clear indicator of national economic trends. For the 2000 recession, expenditures held up remarkably well. While much of the stock market was badly hit, particularly growth stocks, value stocks held up pretty well, only posting a loss of 10.0% in 2002. By contrast, the 2008 recession impacted expenditures dramatically.

The Bureau publishes a report monthly showing Current Income and Expenditures and some seven previous months data. In this way, you can spot trends. In **Table 7** of this report a Sub Heading under Personal Consumption Expenditures is shown. This is for Durable Goods. In the first section, dramatic declines appear in the total expenditures per month and in the following section, the change from the previous month's totals.

Table 3
Real Personal Consumption Expenditures

	Aug 08	Sep 08	Oct 08	Nov 08	Dec 08
			Billions seasonal]		
Personal consumption expenditures	8,269.3	8,231.0	8,167.7	8,196.4	8,147.5
Durable goods	1,200.4	1,161.4	1,101. 9	1,114.2	1,109.8
Nondurable goods	2,378.5	2,358.3	2,325.4	2,337.5	2,292.8
Services	4,703.9	4,713.4	4,724.9	4,732.2	4,731.1
			Change from preceding period		
Personal consumption expenditures	-12.1	-38.3	-63.3	28.7	-48.9
Durable goods	21.9	-39.0	-59.5	12.3	-4.4
Nondurable goods	-13.5	-20.2	-32.9	12.1	-44.7
Services	-12.7	9.5	11.5	7.3	-1.1

I took the Durable Goods expenditures of last quarter of 2007 as a base and how the subsequent quarters shown below compared to it.:

2008
1st Qtr. – 0.9%
2ndQtr -1.7%
3rdQtr -5.6%
4thQtr - 11.2%

2009
1stQtr -10.6%
2ndQtr-14.2%
3rdQtr -10.2%

From then on, the reductions leveled off with the economy showing real progress, though still far from robust.

Conclusions: These are some of the most important highlights leading to the worst recession since the so-called Great Depression of the 1930's. By following these same statistics in the future when there are rumblings in the media about the possibility of another recession you can inform yourself of these trends. With these signals of a downturn, you can make the necessary changes to your portfolio holdings and prevent a significant loss of assets. These reports will show previous months' results for each statistic so that you can spot trends. Frequently, it is recommended that it is best to look at some three months before concluding that there really is a trend. In some cases, such as the Weekly Claims for Unemployment, the changes were so dramatic in the October/November 2008 period, that if you hadn't already taken the steps to exit equity funds into safe harbors, you should have waited no longer to do so. With the benefit of hindsight, one could easily make the case that one should have made the change to a Money Market Fund or Long Term US Treasury Bond Funds in the last quarter of 2007 or the first Quarter of 2008. Without the hindsight, it would be reasonable to conclude from the above Economic Indicators that one should have made the changes say in August 2008. At that point you would have incurred some losses but not nearly to the extent you would have if you stayed in equities throughout the whole down period.

Re-entering the Equity Markets

The first observation to make is that certain economic indicators which best herald an oncoming recession, are not necessarily the same ones to look at when one could safely reenter the equity market. As we have seen in the aftermath of the 2008 recession which officially ended in June 2009, the recovery has been very slow and fitful. A number of pundits may even forecast a so-called double dip recession whereby the economy takes an additional downward plunge. Such forecasts in the past have not subsequently materialized. Nevertheless, there are many periods when the economy simply creeps along the bottom getting neither better nor worse. Keynesian economics, which prescribes extending unemployment benefits which otherwise would expire and direct Government investment in state and local entities, and kick starting infrastructure investments all have a role in preventing even more unemployment and hardship. Political opposition typically takes the form that such assistance is either unnecessary or counterproductive and leading to unsustainable Government debt. Such opposition, which occurred back in the 1930's Great Depression and the most recent recession, often results in terminating such assistance prematurely resulting in lack luster economic performance.

There is little doubt that reemployment results in greatly improved revenues from income and sales and other taxes as people spend their earnings. After World War II, US Government debt as a percentage of GDP was 110%. Factories which turned out tanks, warplanes and other armaments switched back to civilian goods. New growth and the expansion thereby of Government tax revenues resulted in a huge reduction of debt over a 20 year period. As a result, over several years, Government debt as a percentage of GDP declined to far more manageable levels. Clearly, such a strategy of getting more people back to work will ultimately significantly reduce Government debt. By the end of 2010 Government debt was 63% of GDP.

In this relatively uncertain economic climate with continued high unemployment, investors who have parked their money in safe harbors, may wonder when or if they should return to the equity market. Stocks were beaten down very low in the six months from September 2008 through February 2009. Some investors saw this as a golden opportunity to buy such stocks as they were sure they couldn't lose out at such low prices. The market staged a mini rally which failed to presage an overall comeback. The question then comes as to whether small investors should have reentered the Stock Market in this mini rally or stayed put in their safe harbors. Most such investors chose to sit on the sidelines. At this point, there was no clear indication that the economy was on the mend. Unemployment remained stubbornly high. Consumer confidence levels remained low and spending was restricted to buying only essentials. While the Stock Market staged some upticks, there was no compelling indication of a rebound.

Therefore a choice can be made towards staying put – that is keeping your assets in a safe harbor for longer until such an upward trend is more assured, or, go back into equity funds even if their value doesn't increase but simply makes small movements both up and down. You can of course, tiptoe back in by stages so that you are literally in both camps at the same time. This way, any significant downward movement doesn't affect your whole portfolio. As the economy and outlook improves, you can reduce and eventually eliminate the safety of Money Market and/or US Treasuries for Small and Medium Cap Equity Funds.

◇◇◇

The 2000 Recession Recovery

The *Personal Consumption & Expenditure Report* is put out by the Bureau of Economic Analysis (BEA). The monthly reports for the last two quarters of 1999, and all of 2000, 2001, and 2002 showed a small and steady uptick in this area confounding Stock Market free falls in these periods. The NASDAQ was hit the hardest by dropping some 77% from February 28 2000 to the lowest point of 1140 by September 30 2002. As already mentioned, this Exchange was chockfull of tech. stocks which seemed to have been purchased by investors in the late 1990's with little understanding of their prospects. The so called dot.com recession essentially pricked this balloon and investors fled from them in droves. The Dow Jones Average decreased also by 35% from December 31 1999 to a low of 7528 by September 30 2002. While still a very serious drop, it certainly didn't come close to the drop in the NASDAQ. In retrospect, the far larger Dow stocks were much more diversified than the dot.com stocks and were able to weather the storm somewhat better with more traditional offerings of goods and services. The growth stocks were by far the hardest hit – once again were largely the tech stocks. It should be noted that Small Cap Value Funds as a group, were able to produce positive returns for 2000, 2001 and only in 2002 did they lose by a comparatively small amount of 10%. Again in retrospect, compared to the 2008 recession this one should be considered as "Mild."

The *ISM Report*: Though the Stock Market nosedived, especially in tech stocks, in March 2000, the economy as a whole trended downward quite gradually with the ISM Manufacturing Report showing a 54.9 index in March and still 52.5 in July of 2000. Further downshifting occurred for the next 3 months until December when it lowered to 43.9. That continued through July 2001. A modest uptick took place for the rest of the year and January 2002. In February 2002, it was back up to the 50's but then drifted back to the high 40's through June 2003. After that, the recovery took hold and rose through the rest of the year reaching 60.1 in December.

	JAN	FEB	MAR	APR	MAY	JUN	JUL	AUG	SEPT	OCT	NOV	DEC
2003	51.3	48.8	46.3	46.1	49.0	49.0	51.0	53.2	52.4	55.2	58.4	60.1
2002	47.5	50.7	52.4	52.4	53.1	53.6	50.2	50.3	50.5	49.0	48.5	51.6
2001	42.3	42.1	43.1	42.7	41.3	43.2	43.5	46.3	46.2	40.8	44.1	45.3
2000	56.7	55.8	54.9	54.7	53.2	51.4	52.5	49.9	49.7	48.7	48.5	43.9

The 2008 Recession Recovery

As I write, this is still an ongoing process. The automotive industry has staged a dramatic recovery where its production of just 9 million cars in the earliest part of this recession has now risen to 14 million for 2012. This is just 2-3 million lower than its previous peak. New housing starts, which a short time ago seemed just about dead, is finally showing month to month increases.

With the GDP driven by consumer expenditures at 70% of this figure, the signs are pointing to a continuation of slow steady growth.

The Personal Consumption and Expenditure Report: As reported above for the 2000 Recession, this can be a highly important set of data for tracking its severity. In that recession, personal consumption largely continued while Markets went down substantially, particularly the NASDAQ. Small Cap Value Mutual Funds were generally able to escape the carnage. On the other hand, the very high reduction in income and expenditures in the 2008 recession created big drops in all Stock Market indices. The report for April 2009 showed a low of 1.06Billion from a high of 1.26Billion in October 2007 – a reduction of 12%. By the end of 2009, it rose back up to 1.14Billion. By the end of December2010 it rose to 1.24 Billion. The NASDAQ hit a low of 1294 by March 2 2009 and as alluded to above, staged a mini rally later that month rising to 1622 by March 30 2009. By December 28 2009 it was 2269. By December 27 2010 it was 2653.

As I have already emphasized, the obvious strategy with respect to one's portfolio was to switch to Money Market and/or US Long Term Treasuries at some point in 2008, preferably by August of that year. From the data discussed above, one could safely return to equity funds sometime after March 2009. At that point, the PCE Report showed continuing slow increases in that statistic each month thereafter. Though the Stock Market has had ups and downs since then, quite a number of the downs were driven by events overseas such as Greece, Spain and Italy, while our own economy has continued its recovery.

The ISM Report: For the first 7 months of 2009, it rose back up from 34.9 in January to 49.2 in July. A reminder: a reading of 50 for a year would indicate a growth rate of 2.5%. From August 2009 through all of 2010 it registered in the high 50's. A great deal of this improvement was the effects of Government stimulus programs which partially staved off even higher employment and still lower personal spending. The bail-out of the domestic automotive industry saved it from collapse. In 2008 the quantity of cars produced in the USA was a low of 9 million. Currently this number has risen to 14 million. While that is a very significant rebound, one shouldn't forget that the housing market is still very depressed, though as I write it has started to improve. This is an even larger component of the economy and normally a far larger component of the economy than the automotive segment. The latter while staging a remarkable comeback has permanently shed hundreds of thousands of employees and new hires earn substantially less.

	JAN	FEB	MAR	APR	MAY	JUN	JUL	AUG	SEPT	OCT	NOV	DEC
2012	54.1	52.4	53.4	54.8	53.5	49.7	49.8	49.6				
2011	59.9	59.8	59.7	59.7	54.2	55.8	51.4	52.5	52.5	51.8	52.2	53.1
2010	56.7	55.8	59.3	59.0	58.8	56.0	55.7	57.4	56.4	57.0	58.0	57.3
2009	34.9	35.6	36.0	39.8	42.0	45.8	49.2	53.5	54.2	55.9	54.3	55.8
2008	50.3	47.6	48.3	48.8	48.8	49.8	50.0	49.2	44.8	38.9	36.5	33.1

The effect on NASDAQ Composite Index: A partial recovery took the Index back to the 1600-1700's in March and April of 2009. Additional recovery in this Market has taken place again and again only to be aborted by problems in Europe and China. This is an on-going set of problems.

CHAPTER THREE:
COMPARISON OF SMALL VS. LARGE CAP FUNDS, 1999-2010

In Table Four below, I show the individual total returns including dividends and capital gains for both small and Large Cap funds subdivided into Value, Blend (sometimes known as Core) and Growth for the period 1999 through 2010. Since 1929, Small Cap funds have done better due in part to their opportunity to buy and sell stock from among (today's)8300 companies – almost eight times more choices than among the 1074 Large Cap companies. Small Cap funds can cherry pick from this far larger group of companies for superior earnings prospects. Some companies may have a unique niche for a particular product or service. There are 1220 Medium Cap companies. These numbers were reported by the Financial Times. Large Cap companies may well have some new product or service, but the effects on earnings can be muted because of other divisions which may not have a blockbuster new product or service in the same time span. Another advantage for some smaller companies which have devised a new product or service is that they can become takeover targets, which typically raises their stock price. Additionally, of course, when the economy is growing at a significant rate, companies both large and small can profit from greater sales generating higher profits.

Advertisements by mutual funds tend to present statistics which showcase their returns over set periods such as one, three and five years. Such bundling often obscures large each and every one of the twelve years period chosen, you can get a clearer picture of the results of recessions. Such results reinforce my contention that you need to move your fund assets into safe harbors at appropriate times as explained earlier.

In addition to showing the average gains and losses of the various categories of funds, I have included an example whereby a person starts with a $5,000 initial investment and then, on a monthly basis adds $417 a rounded-off amount equal to an additional $5,000/ year. As is the case with mutual funds, the accumulated returns are compounded. All dividends and capital gains are reinvested. You will observe the amount of assets that would be accumulated using the actual percentage returns in each of those 12 years.

Small Cap value funds averaged 9.00%. Blend funds comprising of value and growth stocks came close behind with 8.1%. In periods, when there is not strong growth, this is a good choice of fund because the management of such funds over time may change the proportions of value and growth to take advantage of changes in the economy. Growth funds averaged only 7.10% over the 12 year period. In some years, growth funds have outperformed value or blend. They typically do best when the economy is truly "humming", but do the worst when the opposite is the case. Of course, in all categories, some funds are going to outperform others not only in their own category, but individual funds in other categories.

As previously mentioned, the charts starting on Page 34 show the accumulated assets for 25 years for various rates of return. You can readily observe the large differences which can occur. While the stock markets dictate over all trends, you can work to increase your returns beyond mimicking the category averages.

Table Four.

YEAR	SMALL CAPS						LARGE CAPS					
	VALUE RETURN (%)	INVEST CUM (M)	BLEND RETURN (%)	INVEST CUM (M)	GROWTH RETURN (%)	INVEST CUM (M)	VALUE RETURN (%)	INVEST CUM (M)	BLEND RETURN (%)	INVEST CUM (M)	GROWTH RETURN (%)	INVEST CUM (M)
1999	6.2	10.5	20.3	11.5	56.9	18.2	4.6	10.5	17.7	11.3	40.6	13.1
2000	16.8	17.6	11.5	18.6	-4.3	22.3	9.9	16.7	- 0.8	16.2	-11.8	16.2
2001	18.1	26.3	8.9	25.4	-3.9	26.3	-2.0	21.4	-9.2	19.5	-20.6	17.4
2002	-10.1	28.2	-15.8	26.0	-26.2	23.8	-17.1	22.3	-20.7	20.0	-26.7	17.1
2003	44.8	46.9	43.6	43.4	47.5	41.3	28.3	34.3	27.3	31.1	28.9	27.7
2004	20.6	62.3	18.4	56.8	13.0	52.0	13.2	44.1	10.0	39.4	8.7	35.4
2005	6.7	71.7	7.6	66.3	7.0	60.8	6.0	51.9	5.7	46.8	7.0	43.0
2006	16.2	88.7	15.0	81.7	10.7	72.7	17.7	66.6	14.0	58.7	6.1	50.8
2007	-3.4	90.6	1.1	87.6	9.9	85.2	2.1	73.0	6.9	68.0	15.0	63.8
2008	-33.2	64.7	-35.3	60.8	-41.8	53.5	-36.0	50.8	-36.9	47.0	-40.2	42.1
2009	35.2	93.3	33.9	87.2	36.7	79.1	23.5	68.4	28.0	65.8	35.3	62.9
2010	24.9	122.2	25.6	115.2	27.3	106.4	12.6	82.3	12.7	77.0	14.5	77.4
AVG.	9.0		8.1		7.1		3.5		2.5		2.6	

All the total investment returns were provided by courtesy of Lipper Inc. a Thomson Reuters Co. Although the table uses the term "BLEND," Lipper Inc. prefers the term "CORE." For my purposes, these are the same.

Notes: The funds included above are either No Load or Back Loaded (1% Redemption

Fee). There are no front loaded funds. However, a majority of front loaded funds ("A Class") do offer the alternative of "C Class" – the so-called "Back Loaded" funds.

An Analysis of the Table Above: The total assets invested through the whole 12 year period is $65,000. The span of years chosen show a starting year of 1999 which could be said to be the last year of the roaring nineties with outsize returns. In the following year, the first of the two recessions commenced. The year 2000 ushered in a relatively mild recession relative to 2008. So you have mixture of two recessions and some growth years following 2002– albeit not as robust as the 1990's. Starting in October of 2007 a new downturn in the stockmarkets occurred. Starting in March 2009, the market started to pick up again –fitfully.

With the ever larger global economy and the increased competition, it is difficult to believe that the economic growth of the future will match those years of the nineties.

As already reported above, quite a large number of institutions reporting on mutual funds' history like to group several years together. Some of this is undoubtedly due to a perceived need to simply save space. However, a less than neutral motivation may well be to provide a sort of bromide to the volatility that really exists from one year to the next. . In short, especially for newer investors with less exposure to the vagaries of the market, such groupings clearly mask the huge swings that have occurred in the past and are certain to be repeated in the future. I believe investors need to be aware of year by year history so they under no illusion about it.

Over the entire 12 years, of the three styles of Small Caps, Value funds slightly outshone Blend and particularly Growth. In the 2000 recession which started in March of that year the Value Funds still managed to return a positive 16.8% while the Large Cap Value managed a 9.9% return. Small Cap Growth suffered a 4.3% loss while the Large Cap Growth was down by 11.8%. For 2001 and 2002 Small Caps still did better than Large Caps. Coming out of the recession, Small Caps trumped the Large Caps.

In the recession starting in 2008, all funds got hammered with Small Caps doing only very marginally better than Large Caps. Because of the housing bust and all of its ramifications throughout the economy affecting so many sectors, there was nowhere to hide. Even Value funds were not able to find sufficient niche sectors to stay clear of the recession effects. That was contrary to the 2000 recession when at least in the first year small cap value funds still managed a healthy return.

In that period, there was far more liquidity and consumer expenditures were not so drastically curtailed. Fueling the 2008 recession, consumers had spent a lot of money relying on equity in their housing assets. A great amount was financed by taking out loans based on appreciating house values. When housing values collapsed eventually by 30% or more in many states, this practice came to an abrupt halt. Families have had to hugely rein in their spending, and many owed more on their houses than they were worth. Discretionary spending became so reduced, mortgage holders were unable to make payments so many homeowners were forced into foreclosing on their property. Unemployment skyrocketed to 14 million nationally further roiling financial markets.

Unemployment became the highest since the 1930's recession. The Gross Domestic Product or GDP consisting of the value of all goods and services was reduced by 4%. While that percentage may at first sight not seem like a lot, it amounts to billions of dollars.

CHAPTER FOUR:
401K AND 403B RETIREMENT PLANS

The staples of 401k plans are mutual funds. There are over 7000 of them. However, many such programs even in large companies and institutions offer a highly restricted selection. A common total is about fifteen, especially if you include in the total just one specific age retirement package, out of many listed, with a different proportion of equity and bond funds depending on your age. It will typically include a Small, Medium and Large Cap, a foreign Large Cap fund, and a variety of Corporate and governmental Bonds and a Money Market Bond fund. According to Brightscope, a mutual fund rating organization, some 16% do not include a small cap fund. The funds chosen are usually those of well- known organizations such as Fidelity, American, Vanguard or T. Rowe Price. This immediately confers respectability and security. Because of the huge amount of assets in the funds running into tens of billions of dollars they typically return on the investment about the same as bona fide index funds which make a point of stressing their similarity to the averages for the chosen fund categories.

Employees investing in these categories very frequently choose perceived security over opportunity and risk. For them, Large Cap Funds containing big household name companies represent stability and hoped-for good return on their investment. A perusal of the returns from these large companies for a twelve year period from 199 through 2010 tells a different story. Investors in large growth companies often ended up with slightly more than their inputs over 12 years, meaning market returns were very low. The major factor increasing many investors' holdings is the matching contributions offered by the employer. It may take up to 6% of his or her salary and add 50% to the employee's contribution. So, for example, if an employee each year invests $5,000, the employer would add $2,500. Bond holders might well have earned 3-5% per year in the same time span with far less risk. This is hardly going to take the place of income loss at retirement.

With 401k and 403b programs chosen jointly by employers and the insurance companies, individuals can voluntarily sign up and contribute a set dollar amount each month from a selection of mutual funds. Since the inception of 401k programs in 1983 the older annual allowable contributable amounts for each employee have risen periodically from $1,500 to the some $6,500 a year. These limits are revised periodically and can now (in 2010) run up to $16,500 a year for individuals under 50, and $22,000 for those 50 years and over.

Income Tax Deferral and Roth IRAs

One major provision of mutual funds is the income tax deferral. Your contribution is deducted from your gross income and not taxed at that point. However if you withdraw part or all of your assets, this has to be reported as income and liable to be taxed. Another way to avoid tax liability down the road with, hopefully, greatly increased value, is to convert the assets immediately from the Traditional IRA into a Roth IRA. This way, you will pay income taxes on this conversion, but none thereafter. No matter how much you subsequently earn on your Roth IRAs it will not additionally be taxed. I had already accumulated Traditional IRAs when the Roth IRA program was introduced in 1996 and to ease individuals into the program, one was allowed to pay the taxes on the then current value over a four year period. My wife continued to work for three years after my retirement and her IRAs were all Traditional. It so happened that other mutual funds we owned in non-IRAs created dividends and capital gains which of course had to be included in our tax returns as part of over-all income. At that time, we had insufficient deductions to offset these gains. Then, in 2001 and 2002 following retirement somewhat earlier, taxable income was greatly offset by so called "carry-forward" fund losses from the year 2000 (first recession year) along with other allowable deductions. We were then able to convert a sizable portion of her Traditional IRAs to Roth IRAs with no or low tax liability even though the convertible amount has to be entered as income on the 1040A. The point I wish to make is that as an alternative to converting all contributions immediately to Roth IRAs, an option is to wait for particular years before or after retirement when you have an opportunity to offset the potential tax liability with unusually large legal deductions. You can completely choose the amount and timing so that you can convert by stages rather than all at once. By making partial conversions, you can avoid hefty liabilities for any single tax year. For individuals simply changing funds from one fund company to another, the exchanges must be completed within a 60 day period otherwise the amount will be taxed as a permanent distribution.

Matching Provisions

There is no question that matching contributions will jumpstart an individual's total assets especially in the earlier years of annual contributions to the program. Equally true is that as the years roll by, the matching contributions add a diminishing percentage to the total assets accumulated. By contrast, the total annual returns from capital gains and dividends reinvested assume greater importance. It is therefore particularly crucial to have the assets invested in the most profitable categories. As I have argued, those categories – most of the time – should be Small and Medium Cap funds. While the fund choices offered by companies and institutions generally are very large in assets, and therefore their investment returns are usually similar to index funds, the Small and Medium Cap Fundsare still the better choice over Large Cap funds.

I did some research on exiting 401k mutual funds with the idea that holders of IRAs could do a lot better. While this can be the case, with proper selection and monitoring, the fact is that the matching feature, for as long as it is offered, provides a more assured cushion even with the lowered returns vs. managed IRAs. However, usually the 401k program has a cap where maybe it takes effect on up to say 6% of an individual's salary. For example, an individual whose salary is $80,000/yr. would be entitled to a 50% matching amount on $4,800 which is $2,400. If the employee wishes to save more than that, in other words, without the matching provision, an option would be to open an IRA opting for higher return funds rather than the restricted fund offerings in the 401k program.

Individuals in 403b programs typically do not have a matching provision. If the mutual fund offerings seem too limited, such investors may wish to explore the far wider world of funds available with IRAs and the returns one might reasonably expect from some of the better ones. Some of these 403b programs demand exit fees of up to 7% which could be quite a deterrent to making such a change. One alternative to look at would be to freeze further contributions to one's existing program, and only invest future contributions into IRAs. Every IRA allows for automatic regular monthly contributions which can be made via your bank. One small drawback, would be that rather than reducing your tax liability each month as you would in your 403b program, you would have to wait to receive that after submitting your annual 1040 returns. On a cost of money basis, this could penalize you to probably less than a $100 a year which could be a small price to pay vs. the accumulated higher returns from your fund(s) selections over a number of years.

CHAPTER FIVE:
INVESTING IN IRA'S WITH THE HELP OF MORNINGSTAR

General

Despite a lot of evidence highlighting problems with these 401k and 403b programs held by millions, there is no doubt that many individuals will continue to invest in them because they may feel uncomfortable in stepping outside of them into other entities such as IRA's. The most important change by far is to retreat out of equity funds before a recession really gets underway.

I will examine various aspects of doing your own research on funds to best profit from them and awareness of tactics that can diminish your returns. I would recommend that over time you invest in some three or four funds at a minimum.

Your goal in selecting funds should be to choose those whose performance in the last 12 months and year to date (if at least 3 months have passed) is in the upper 15%. Morningstar provides such rankings for each of the funds in any category so this information is very readily available. They provide a ranking out of 100. Much like the traditional bell shaped curve, the majority of funds will hover on each side of the average of 50. Obviously, if you select funds in this average area, you are likely to reap just that – average returns on your investment. However by selecting funds in the upper 15% in ranking does not guarantee continued ranking in that realm. My research shows that about 60% of funds manage to stay in the top 25% for a year. That means if you chose let's say four funds, one or two of them are likely to fall below that, some even into the lower 50%. By frequently checking the rankings of the chosen funds within the same category you can avoid further lowering of returns in your overall portfolio by switching out of these funds and into new ones.

You may say that is a lot of bother to go through. Why do it? The answer is that the return on funds which manage to stay in the top 25% of their peers will return 3% more than the average. If you can stay in the top 15% (obviously a tougher goal) your return can be 6% more than the average. I have previously shown that Small Cap Value Funds averaged a 9.0% return over a 12 year period even when continuing in them during recessions. So by carefully monitoring your portfolio and willingness to switch funds periodically, you could have produced a 12.0% return. By even more diligence, and may be a little luck, if you managed to stay in the top 15% you could have produced a 15.0% return. I have found that these differences persisted among funds even when the overall category performance was lower in any one year than the 12 year average of 9.0%.

A word about making fund selections. As of 2010, there were 75 Small Value Funds, 164 Blend and 101 Growth small caps. That is a total of 340 funds. Note: These numbers only include "C" and" No Load" Class funds. Mathematics would indicate that there are about 75 funds collectively which would constitute the upper 25% by ranking of the total of 340 funds and almost 50 funds in the upper 15% ranking.

You will find that it is helpful to print out the Quote, Performance and Holdings pages of funds in a particular category you are interested in. This way, if you select, let's say, half a dozen funds in this manner even though you may be only after a single final selection, you will be able later to compare them side by side instead of relying upon your memory.

Navigating Morningstar to Aid Fund Selection

A toolbar on Morningstar's, Website will show among other titles, Stocks, Funds etc. Click on Funds and after getting to that section, scroll down the page until you see Premium Fund Screens and Basic screens. If you become a paid member of Morningstar you can observe analysts' reports if they exist for various funds. If you are not a member, the basic screens still provide you with a ton of information on each fund.

Click on Basic Screens, and a Box will pop up with invitations to visit Domestic and International Funds. Click on Domestic and the next box brings up a whole raft of Bond and Equity Funds. Let's say you select Small Cap Value Funds. Click on it.

Scroll on down this page and you can limit your search by requiring that the manager has been in charge for X number of years or more. I, personally, don't immediately limit my search by preempting one's search by this factor. Later on, you may wish to pass judgment on this issue. Scroll down still more and check each of the one to five stars. At this beginning point you may want to take a peek at all starred funds in their alphabetical order. However, because particular funds may be in three or more classes, the 25 fund total on each page may actually cover only eight different funds by their common investments.(See discussion of classes, above.). Morningstar limits your category selection to 200 funds total. After, say, a first time look for funds with better than average performance, page by page, you may well have reached the 200 fund total (some eight pages) before coming to the end of the alphabet. To be able to scan those funds at the upper end of the alphabet you can go back to the very first page and eliminate one and/ or two star funds by unchecking them. You can, if you prefer, scan through to all funds one starred group at a time. Either of these two ways will enable you to get to the end of the alphabet.

What to Look for in Morningstar Screens

Performance. Performance is probably the first and most important factor to look at. As you would expect, a screen will show the current 12 month total return for each fund. While most are similar to the average, a few will stand out by two or three percentage points or more higher. The fund titles which appear don't immediately show the class. To observe that, click on essentially the same fund by assets and by similar performance. A pop-up will quickly allow you to discover whether they have a "C" Class or not. Click on "Quote." This page will bring up lots of useful additional information. In the "Quote" toolbar, it will indicate whether the fund is "No Load" or "Load". For more specific info. you can again go to a sub Toolbar to "Performance" and see how the fund has fared in previous years and, very importantly, how it compared with the category averages in those years. CAUTION. Almost without exception, the better funds do worse than others during the first year of a recession as they have further to fall from their lofty height leading up to it. This is an admonition previously discussed.

Ranking. A fund's ranking compared to its peers is an excellent measure of its performance. A ranking of around 50 (out of 100) means it is just average – with half the other funds doing better, while the other half does worse. Near the top of the scale, a ranking of 10 (that is better than 90 other funds) will help you make your selection. While the fund's stock picking always has elements of "luck", the fact that it has chosen anywhere from 50 to 200 companies in its portfolio ensures that its total return does truly represent some real expertise over its rivals. Of course, part of its success can derive from the chosen sector weights. If the fund's manager chooses a higher sector weighting in a sector (such as energy) which is trending higher than in those of other funds, that will give it a boost in the rankings. That choice is, of course available to other fund managers. Some funds simply believe that they do not want to put too many eggs in just a few sectors and prefer to operate more conservatively by spreading their holdings more evenly over many other sectors. It is also a good idea to observe whether outside of a recession year (such as 2008) a particular fund or funds had a high ranking in several previous years.

Star Ratings. While, Morningstar's ratings system can be useful in reducing the number of funds to be reviewed by only checking funds with say a 4 or 5 Star Rating, you may wish to see if there are a few 3 Star funds which deserve a closer look. Some of the time, a fund may change managers and start to improve the results over the previous manager. Understandably, before amending a star rating upwards, Morningstar may wait to see if the improvement continues or is just a flash in the pan, so to speak.

Fees. These relate to the fees charged by the fund for carrying out the selection of stocks and various administrative expenses. For equity funds, these are usually in the 1.25% to 1.50% range. Some of the time, they are higher, and Morningstar will deduct points in their Ratings process because of higher fees. Nevertheless, I have found that better performance can occur because of maybe more research or more skilled stock pickers. If a fund can make say 3% more than many of its rivals, why should I complain if it comes at a 0.5% higher expense?

Price/Earnings Ratios. Take a look at Price/Earnings ratios. Morningstar looks at the latest stock portfolio of the fund and checks their current price against its earnings. A low P/E ratio is desirable, a high one undesirable. For example, a P/E ratio of 12 means that the average price of a fund's stock portfolio would return $8.33 for each $1 of investment (100 div.by 12). Conversely, a P/E of 24 would return only $4.17 for each $1 of investment (100 div.by 24). Morningstar has to arrive at a composite average for the entire portfolio. Value fund managers in particular are adept at finding stocks which in their opinion are currently undervalued and expect their future value to increase. Growth stock funds are focused on companies poised for anticipated expansion and associated higher earnings and are somewhat less concerned about P/E ratios (which if their predictions come true) may lower the P/E ratios. At the beginning of periods following a recession, value funds tend to shine as most stocks have taken a beating and it is easier to find gems. Growth funds may take longer to catch fire but can outclass their Value fund rivals when the economy is clearly accelerating. Conversely when the economy seems to be teetering at the top of a growth cycle, growth funds tend to falter and may well start downhill.

Holdings. A feature to look at is a list of the top group of stocks accounting for maybe 20-50% of the portfolio. Morningstar calculates the percentage a particular stock holding is of the total fund assets and is displayed along with its latest earnings gain or loss percentage. Naturally, it is best that the greater majority of holdings show decent gains and far fewer with losses. By this means you can check whether the superior overall performance is the result of a successful largish group of stock choices in the portfolio rather than one or two blockbusters. Some portfolios are concentrated among relatively few companies while others have many more. The concentrated portfolio is more likely to show higher gains at the expense of safety and greater volatility.

Sector Weights. Another aspect to take note of is the fund's sector weighting. Morningstar breaks down the current sector weighting of each fund. Sectors include financial, health, technology, materials, energy, real estate and a number of others. At any one time, the Market may favor or disfavor a particular sector. The fund's current success over its rivals may well depend on its ownership of higher weightings of a particular sector(s). This is an area where astute portfolio managers can move around their stock pickings to take advantage of trend changes.

Fund Turnover. At the top of Morningstar's Quote page you will observe a fund's stock turnover rate. This is the frequency of making stock changes in the course of a year. This statistic can be all over the map. Most often, a fund will make such changes from 50 to 100 times. This is pretty normal. A few funds may switch fewer than 25 times. This can mean their stock selections were so good when they made them that they see no reason to change them. They may also believe that in the longer term their patience will be rewarded. At the other end of the scale a few funds may trade almost daily looking for short term gains. In short, there are a variety of investing styles, and all the prospective investor can do is observe the funds' success and reward those that do the best by offering your assets for inclusion in their fund.

Asset Size. Generally, the funds which are relatively small in assets have the opportunity to obtain superior returns. As time goes by, if their returns are very good, some funds will attract more investors. They will then have more assets to manage which may make company selection for the best returns more problematic. With the superior small caps funds, this can start to dilute these better returns from previous cherry picked companies and their selections of additional companies for their portfolio can result in diluting their stellar returns. I like to pick funds that are maybe $50 million+ but maybe less than $600 million in assets. Now there are one or two well-known fund families which have much larger portfolios that manage to beat the odds. I can only assume that they have the where-with-all to conduct superior research compared to rivals and are able to maintain their superior status. What some fund companies do is to close a fund to new investors in order to limit its size and avoid the pitfalls I just described.

Fund Manager's Tenure. One feature Morningstar tracks is the length of the Manager's tenure with the fund. Way back in the 1980's, Peter Lynch ran Fidelity's Large Cap Magellan Fund and its success prompted him to fame. The stock market exploded in this period and one could make very good returns almost regardless of the category or categories you were in. The Magellan Fund reached some 100 Billion in assets, the largest in the country, and then the returns started to erode. In the more recent past, for truly wealthy individuals, Hedge Funds have become the chosen vehicles. In their initial years of operation, hedge funds produced outsize returns for their investors. Even during recessions, by means of "shorting" (not available to equity stocks in mutual funds) they could make money for their investors – at least in the earlier stages. More recent returns have averaged 6 to 8%. For truly wealthy investors – a perfectly adequate return but hardly outstanding.

Other Fund Categories

Sector Funds. At various times, Sector Funds, which specialize in certain parts of the economy such as finance, health, energy, natural resources, and real estate to name just some of those offered, may perform very well, outshining more generalized funds as discussed above. The inherent concern is that their very success in earnings and share price gains will cease to continue for later periods of time. When share prices seem to have crested, a so-called correction may set in which may wipe out some or all previous gains.

International Funds. For many years, I invested in a number of international funds and most of the time the investment returns were quite rewarding. This was especially true when the dollar was declining in relation to other currencies. At the same time, emerging economies were taking off and producing stellar growth and reported profits. Now with the US dollar appreciating significantly in value against these other currencies the funds invest in, the overall value of the fund can be adversely affected regardless of the positive performance of the foreign companies' stocks. The situation can worsen if the international fund invests all its assets in a single country's stocks. However, it should be added that changes in currency valuations typically occur fairly gradually so there is ample time to move out of such funds as currency valuations change in an adverse direction to the US dollar. Some funds will invest in either small or large cap companies, the equivalent of our so called blue chip companies. In short, they have a good history of superior management and consistent profitability.

CHAPTER SIX:
REGULAR MONITORING OF AN INVESTMENT PORTFOLIO

In the old days, in 401k programs, and before the advent of computers and companies such as Morningstar, one relied on quarterly reports from the Company's Administrator, an insurance company, to show you how your investments performed in that quarter. Fortunately, most of the time, the results were very encouraging so no action was called for. You could treat it as you might a bank account—passively.

I would argue that today such a strategy is completely outmoded because of more frequent recessions and the need to be far more proactive in one's investments.

Whether you continue with your 401k program as is, or freeze it, as you can without penalty, or simply as an adjunct to it, you can enjoy the huge advantage of choice in IRAs particularly in Small Caps both domestic and international. Most companies offering 401k programs choose well known purveyors of funds which in turn grow even larger with returns similar to index funds – that is to say average.

While I have shown that over a recent 12 year period, domestic Small Cap Value funds have averaged some 9.0% compounded even through there were two recessions in the period, by following various steps, you can boost your returns quite significantly.

The first step is to decide in rough terms where the current business cycle is. Is the economy clearly in the "up" part with no real peak observable, at a peak, or teetering on a downward trend, the bottom of a recession, a "bottom" or possibly, fitful upturn. The answer to those questions should dictate where you should be depositing your money. In a recessionary environment you need to stay out of equity funds. In this phase you are essentially safeguarding your assets rather than risk further drops in value. When it appears the economy is at the end of a downturn, you can tiptoe into equity funds, may be keeping some assets in money market funds until an upturn is clearly established. At that point, you can progressively move towards equity funds.

In the first stages of a recession recovery, Value funds both Small and Medium tend to shine as the market has previously beaten them down. Their underlying strength starts to shine through, their value is realized and share prices recover. Depending on the length and depth of the recession, growth funds may take longer to recover. Blend funds containing both value and growth stocks may well be a good choice during this interim period. As the economy improves such funds may well tend to contain a greater segment of growth to value stocks. What an investor can do is regularly check all Morningstar's three small cap screens and at the bottom of any page they print the current year to date averages for each. This way you can follow the trends of each category as the year progresses. This is not to rule out an investment in a fund which is not in the most rewarding group. However it does suggest a greater likelihood of finding more funds currently producing better returns.

I have tended to stress Small Cap funds as the best category to obtain better results. As some such funds get bigger, they often look for additional returns among medium size companies, whose capitalization is between $1 and $10 Billion in assets. Once again, the Medium size Value Funds tend to lead the way from recessions with Growth and Blend funds recovering later. Some funds include the word medium or an abbreviation of it in its title. Morningstar shows for each fund, a box with a weighted mid-point for the funds' assets as they may veer between value, blend and growth and small, medium and large companies. I should add that Morningstar may well study a fund company's assets and decide that their title no longer reflects what their current stance is and state in their quotation that despite the title word "value" they may operate more, for example, as a "blend" fund.

There are a number of home or personal financial software packages in the market place which enables one to monitor your financial affairs keeping track of all such transactions such as income(s) mortgage and car payments, utilities, and all other expenses. Many people find it very useful to monitor these financial transactions to better keep track of them and make monthly payments through instructions to their bank, etc. The more transactions you have the more incentive there is to use such packages. Being retired, I personally have fewer transactions and use just the investment segment of the software. I have only used Quicken's package for many years and find it extremely useful. Every few years they obsolete a particular year's package and will not support older editions.

Like a lot of software, it takes a while to get used to it and get the most out of it but the end result can be particularly rewarding. You enter each of the funds you own to include obviously its name, and you will be prompted to enter the number of shares owned, price paid per share which of course when multiplied out is your initial investment. You will need to add columns for market value and year to date % return. You may want to add the day's % return. There are many additional options you can include. Each trading day after 6.00pm you can click on Quicken to bring up your portfolio. A company named Comstock whom Quicken has a contract with, will at your prompt, update your portfolio and you can immediately see whether you gained or lost from the previous day. To come out ahead, you have to be prepared for both gains and losses. One can guarantee that even in an overall market upswing you will have many days when you incur losses. Each daily snapshot will enable you to spot both market trends and the performance of individual funds. While some funds may exceed expectations others may disappoint.

If you haven't closely followed economic trends and day to day events which affect the stock market – welcome to Wall Street! It can be particularly galling to hear that the market had a down day, for instance, because the sale of bonds in Spain didn't fare as well as expected or some other event which seems to have absolutely no direct bearing on the health of the funds you chose. In addition, you are very much at the mercy of hedge funds which on any given day expect to see a rise or fall and make money either way as long as they guessed right. In the longer run, a company's share price will depend on real prospects of gain or loss and ultimately be reflected in the value of your funds' assets in that company.

I usually give funds in my portfolio a couple of months to compare with their category peers. If they rise or fall in tandem, it is usually the market. If a fund or funds, compare less well, and by that I mean are say 3% lower than their peers, maybe it is time to go back to the Morningstar's screens and take a look at other funds. Frequently, check to see how your fund's year to date compares to the averages and to other funds. Assuming you are dealing directly with them, the redemption procedure of your fund differs from one fund company to another. Provided you have included a voided bank check with your initial application, a telephone call to their Customer Service department may be all that is necessary to execute your request. Other fund companies may want you to fill out a Distribution Form which you can often download from their web site and then send to them or they may want a letter from you which has a bank green Signature Guarantee stamp verifying the authenticity of your signature. A notarized signature is not acceptable. Brokerages will execute trades very promptly. Reinvestment must take place within 60 days otherwise the IRS will tax your IRA distribution. A brokerage may indicate that they cannot offer a particular fund's "C" Class. Do not get an "A" Class but find an alternative "C" Class fund.

CHAPTER SEVEN:
CHARTS SHOWING ACCUMULATED SAVINGS DEPENDENT ON INVESTMENT RETURNS

On the following pages, if you are in a 401k or 403b program, you can track what your yearly investment return has averaged from inception in the plan.

In order to use the Charts, you would need to make adjustments to two factors in your own situation in order to make them comparable First of all is the initial $5,000 investment in the Charts. This figure was included for IRA plans as you cannot start in them from zero as you can in 401k and 403b plans. A simple adjustment for those in such plans is simply to subtract a year to the number of years you have actually been in your 401k or 403b plan. That way you have essentially subtracted one year's contribution in the charts to make them equal. For individuals who have made varying contributions the best you can do is average them. Next, if your average yearly contribution is less or more than $5,000 you will need to divide it into that number to make it compatible. Then with the number of years you have been in your plan plus one, multiplied by your accumulated savings at the previous year's end adjusted by the factor derived from your contribution comparison you can see what percentage you have been able to earn.

For example. John has been in his 401k plan for 7 years.

> Actual Accumulated Savings = $34,864
> Calculation: 7 - 1 = 6 years
> > $5,000 (Chart) divided by $4,000 (John) = 1.25
> > Chart Accumulated Savings = $34,864 x 1.25= $43,580
> > Average Percentage Return = 6.0% approx..

It is frequently mentioned that to maintain your standard of living in retirement, you need to take your new found social security entitlements and then add earnings from invested assets to supply roughly a total of 2/3rds of your previous employment income. Of course, your retirement may coincide with the end of mortgage payments so that can impact your expenditures in a significant way. You may drive far less. On the other hand, out of pocket medical costs may increase. There are numerous changes both up and down. As mentioned earlier, it is usually recommended that you use only 4-6% of your investable assets from year to year. By that yardstick, you can make some rough estimates of what assets you will need to accumulate during, say a 25 year period, as shown in the Charts. You will also be able to observe what rate of return leading up to the beginning of retirement and beyond. Unless you become severely incapacitated, is there any reason to believe you cannot be just as capable of investing your money as wisely as before?

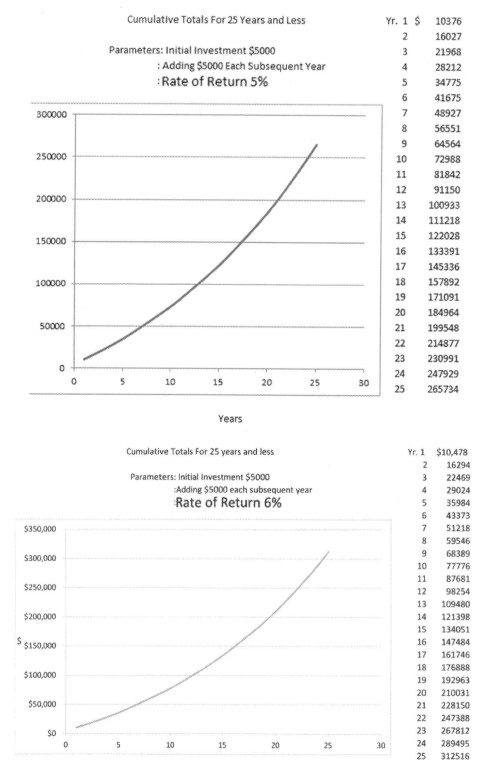

Cumulative Totals For 25 Years and Less

Parameters: Initial Investment $5000
: Adding $5000 Each Subsequent Year
:Rate of Return 5%

Years

Yr. 1	$	10376
2		16027
3		21968
4		28212
5		34775
6		41675
7		48927
8		56551
9		64564
10		72988
11		81842
12		91150
13		100933
14		111218
15		122028
16		133391
17		145336
18		157892
19		171091
20		184964
21		199548
22		214877
23		230991
24		247929
25		265734

Cumulative Totals For 25 years and less

Parameters: Initial Investment $5000
:Adding $5000 each subsequent year
Rate of Return 6%

Years

Yr. 1	$10,478
2	16294
3	22469
4	29024
5	35984
6	43373
7	51218
8	59546
9	68389
10	77776
11	87681
12	98254
13	109480
14	121398
15	134051
16	147484
17	161746
18	176888
19	192963
20	210031
21	228150
22	247388
23	267812
24	289495
25	312516

Cumulative Totals For 25 Years and Less

Parameters: Initial Investment $5000
: Adding $5000 Each Subsequent Year
:Rate of Return 7%

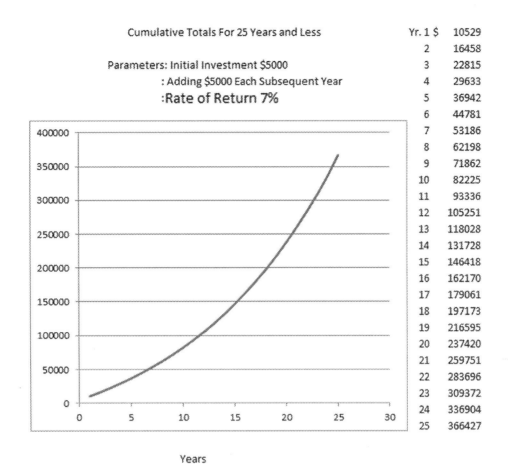

Years

Yr. 1 $	10529
2	16458
3	22815
4	29633
5	36942
6	44781
7	53186
8	62198
9	71862
10	82225
11	93336
12	105251
13	118028
14	131728
15	146418
16	162170
17	179061
18	197173
19	216595
20	237420
21	259751
22	283696
23	309372
24	336904
25	366427

Cumulative Totals for 25 Years and Less

Parameters: Initial Iinvestment $5000
: Adding $5000 Each Subsequent Year
: Rate of Return 8%

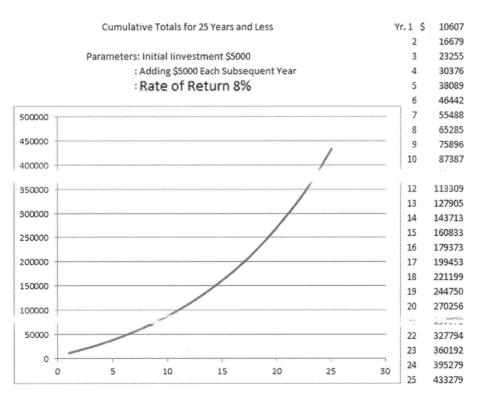

Years

Yr. 1 $	10607
2	16679
3	23255
4	30376
5	38089
6	46442
7	55488
8	65285
9	75896
10	87387
12	113309
13	127905
14	143713
15	160833
16	179373
17	199453
18	221199
19	244750
20	270256
22	327794
23	360192
24	395279
25	433279

35

Cumulative Totals For 25 Years and Less

Parameters: Initial Investment $5000
: Adding $5000 Each Subsequent Year
:Rate of Return 9%

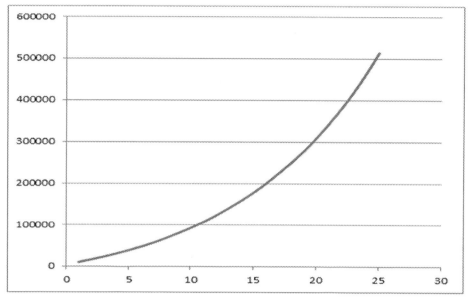

Years

Yr.	$
1	10685
2	16903
3	23704
4	31143
5	39280
6	48181
7	57916
8	68565
9	80212
10	92952
11	106887
12	122130
13	138802
14	157038
15	176985
16	198804
17	222668
18	248772
19	277324
20	308555
21	342715
22	380079
23	420949
24	465653
25	514550

Cumulative Totals For 25 years and less

Parameters: Initial Investment $5000
: Adding $5000 each subsequent year
:Rate of Return : 10 %

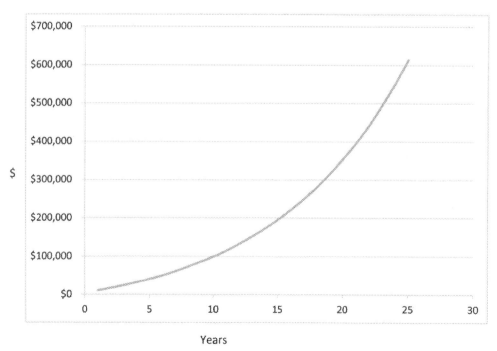

Years

Yr.	$
1	$10,807
2	17222
3	24309
4	32138
5	40787
6	50341
7	60896
8	72556
9	85437
10	98956
11	114557
12	131793
13	150933
14	171867
15	195104
16	220773
17	249131
18	280458
19	315066
20	353297
21	395531
22	442189
23	493732
24	550672
25	613574

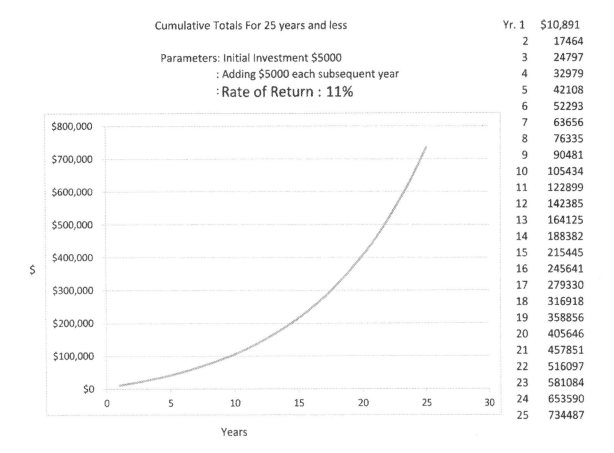

Cumulative Totals For 25 years and less

Parameters: Initial Investment $5000
: Adding $5000 each subsequent year
: Rate of Return : 11%

Yr. 1	$10,891
2	17464
3	24797
4	32979
5	42108
6	52293
7	63656
8	76335
9	90481
10	105434
11	122899
12	142385
13	164125
14	188382
15	215445
16	245641
17	279330
18	316918
19	358856
20	405646
21	457851
22	516097
23	581084
24	653590
25	734487

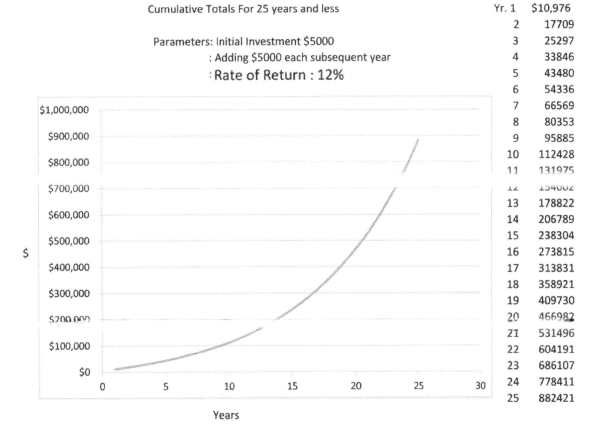

Cumulative Totals For 25 years and less

Parameters: Initial Investment $5000
: Adding $5000 each subsequent year
: Rate of Return : 12%

Yr. 1	$10,976
2	17709
3	25297
4	33846
5	43480
6	54336
7	66569
8	80353
9	95885
10	112428
11	131975
12	154002
13	178822
14	206789
15	238304
16	273815
17	313831
18	358921
19	409730
20	466982
21	531496
22	604191
23	686107
24	778411
25	882421

Cumulative Totals For 25 years and less

Parameters: Initial Investment $5000
: Adding $5000 each subsequent year
:Rate of Return : 13%

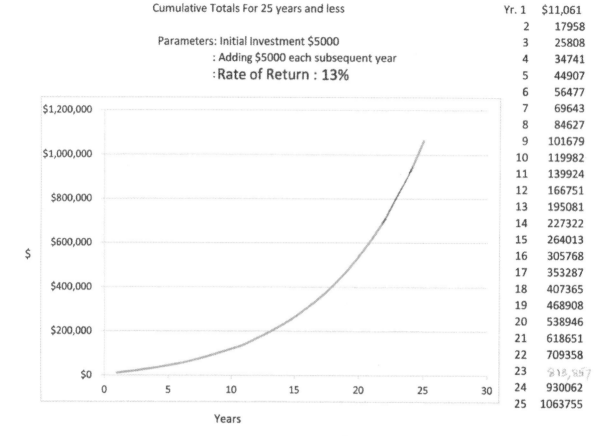

Yr.	
Yr. 1	$11,061
2	17958
3	25808
4	34741
5	44907
6	56477
7	69643
8	84627
9	101679
10	119982
11	139924
12	166751
13	195081
14	227322
15	264013
16	305768
17	353287
18	407365
19	468908
20	538946
21	618651
22	709358
23	815,857
24	930062
25	1063755

Cumulative Totals For 25 years and less

Parameters: Initial Investment $5000
:Adding $5000 each subsequent year
:Rate of Return 14%

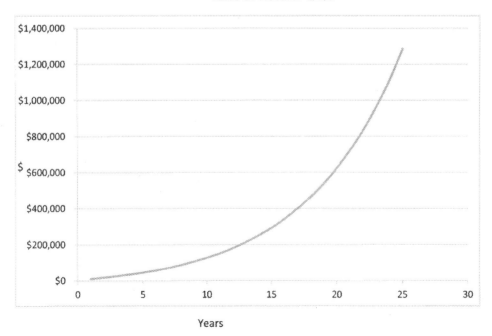

Yr.	
Yr. 1	$11,085
2	18078
3	26116
4	35354
5	45971
6	58174
7	72201
8	88321
9	106849
10	128144
11	152619
12	180750
13	213081
14	250241
15	292950
16	342038
17	398457
18	463301
19	537829
20	623488
21	721938
22	835092
23	965144
24	1110353
25	1286416

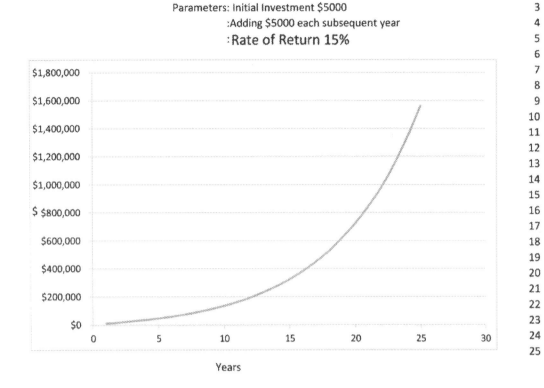

Cumulative Totals For 25 years and less

Parameters: Initial Investment $5000
:Adding $5000 each subsequent year
:Rate of Return 15%

Yr.	
Yr. 1	$11,167
2	18324
3	26633
4	36277
5	47471
6	60466
7	75548
8	93056
9	113378
10	136967
11	164347
12	196130
13	233021
14	275843
15	325549
16	383245
17	450216
18	527954
19	618187
20	722926
21	844503
22	985623
23	1149430
24	1339568
25	1560272

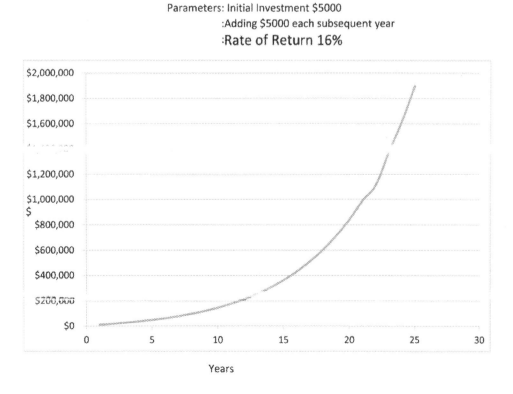

Cumulative Totals For 25 years and less

Parameters: Initial Investment $5000
:Adding $5000 each subsequent year
:Rate of Return 16%

Yr.	
Yr. 1	$11,249
2	18575
3	27162
4	37230
5	49031
6	62865
7	79083
8	98094
9	120381
10	146507
11	177133
12	
13	255123
14	304462
15	362299
16	430101
17	509582
18	602756
19	711981
20	840022
21	990121
22	1116078
23	1372347
24	1614150
25	1897609

EPILOGUE

Since the 2008 Recession, a number of Congressional Committee hearings have taken place discussing the effects of the recession on the devastating effects for employees' Retirement Savings in 401k programs and for retirees in general. Among the worst individuals affected are those near to retirement who counted on these nest eggs to supplement Social Security payouts. Many individuals saw these assets reduced by 40 – 50 %. Being so close to retirement, meant they had too short a time opportunity to recover their assets by a continuation of contributions to their employee retirement programs.

The globalization of trade and world -wide competition has made U.S. companies phase out traditionally defined benefit plans once commonly offered for employees as they already have a hard time competing against foreign rivals. Instead they have turned to 401k programs with a much lower cost to administer even with matching provisions vs. the defined benefit plans. Therefore these Congressional hearings will not attempt to bring back these older more costly plans.

Brokerage representatives have been asked to provide better guidance for investors as they often failed to protect them from the ravages of the recession. Language in their charter refers only to the requirement to offer "suitable" investment advice rather than a more direct requirement of "best" advice. So far, they have successfully resisted changing their mission.

What I have tried to do is to educate investors to be able to detect likely coming recessions and what actions to take to protect their assets.

I do believe that one doable change to 401k programs which would be very beneficial, would be to offer full freedom for members to invest in any mutual funds they chose to rather than the highly restricted group typically offered. Insurance companies sponsoring these programs would inevitably cry that such changes would increase the costs of administering them. While granting that may well be the case, the potential for members to improve their returns especially over time could be very rewarding. One possibility which could be explored would be for insurance companies to offer a two tier program whereby the first tier would be to offer a traditional set-up with a small number of funds to choose

41

from with a second tier which would cost more to members but allow them unlimited selection of funds. For members unwilling to invest time and effort into potentially more remunerative funds, the lower cost funds and likely lower returns might well be their choice, while for others the opposite would be the case. Should members choosing either course change their minds over time, there should be a provision to switch plans.